#Am I Next?

a poetic movement for political reform & Black liberation

Tytianna Ringstaff, PhD

This book is dedicated to my brother, Michael Tyler Perry, my hero.

Copyright © 2020 by Dr. Tytianna N. M. Ringstaff
ISBN: 978-0-9910318-8-7

All rights reserved. No part of this book may be used or reproduced in any manner whatsoever without written permission.

Cover Art by: Daphne Walker

For information on book purchases, readings, & speaking inquiries, please contact:

Honey Tree Publishing
www.honeytreepublishingus.com
honeytreepublishingus@gmail.com

Printed in the United States of America

preface

All poems and artistic expressions in this book are original and primary texts that I collected during the post-Civil Rights era from January through July 2020 during the Covid19 (Coronavirus) global pandemic.

During this difficult moment in history, lives were not only lost all over the world due to the Coronavirus but to institutional and structural racism exercised by the Fraternal Order of Police (FOP) in the United States with the genocide of Black lives through police shootings of innocent Black persons. Four shootings in particular, including Ahmaud Arbery, Breonna Taylor, George Floyd, David McAtee, sparked an outcry for police reform, peace, justice, solidarity, and unity throughout the world.

This book is in memory of Ahmaud Arbery, Breonna Taylor, George Floyd, David McAtee, & countless Black lives that have been lost to police brutality all in the name of racism.

With the efforts of community activists on every platform and all over the world, including members of Keepers of the Torch, a clandestine collective of concerned Black community members in Louisville, Kentucky, that I launched with three brothers, we have seen policy change planted at the grassroots level and manifested into legislation. Particularly, Breonna's Law (banned No-Knock Warrants) was enacted on Thursday, June 12th, 2020. Breonna Taylor was a young Black EMT worker in Louisville, Kentucky, who was shot to death more than eight times in her home by the FOP.

This book is a record of my art and activism during the 2020 Global Pandemic that changed the course of history.

introduction

The **#AmINext?** Movement, born during my journey and mission to help dismantle violence against Black men and women on a global level, is an artistic, political, and cultural movement that gives voice to Black women and men who are victims and survivors of various manifestations of violence.

My brother, Michael, is a survivor of gun violence. On September 13th, 2019, an unknown man loitered on our family property. My brother advised him to leave the premises. However, unexpectedly, the unknown man senselessly retaliated by shooting at my brother. In self-defense, my brother returned fire and a shootout ensued on the street until the unknown man was out of sight. Shortly afterward, my brother was shot twice, shattering the bone in his left arm and puncturing the main artery in his left leg. When my brother tried to get help while losing consciousness in the street, two police officers arrived on the scene but disregarded his life-threatening injuries. Despite the severity of his wounds, the two officers called a third officer who eventually helped him. However, the first two officers should have immediately responded due to my brother's critical condition.

Thankfully, Michael, my brother, and hero who protected me and our family home, survived this horrendous experience and his life was spared. For two weeks, he lived in the intensive care unit (ICU) where I stayed with him. However, not many with gunshot wounds are survivors like my brother and leave the ICU alive. He didn't deserve that. No one does. No one deserves to get a call that their loved one has been shot. No one deserves to clean their loved one's blood off the streets. No one should have to go through that.

While I helped my brother with his wounds, mine were still weeping. The morning after the shooting, on September 14th, a news story about a man who had committed sexual crimes against women at a prestigious company aired on the T.V. in the hospital room. I listened but my mind was too foggy from all that had happened to my brother to recognize the connection. It wasn't until I left the hospital to drive to a meeting for my doctoral program that I got a phone call from my mother who had also seen the news report.

"Did you see on the news that some man is under investigation for sexually assaulting women?" my Momma asked.

My eyes grew large and widely searched the streets around me to understand all that my Momma was saying. She was alluding to an incident I had shared with her about a man who had sexually assaulted me a few months prior. I wasn't sure if it was him under investigation, but I was about to find out.

After I finished the call with my mother, I searched for and found the news article. Three unidentified women had filed lawsuits against this predator. It was the same man who sexually assaulted me. Reading the news article, I immediately grew disgusted and angry all over again about the sexual assault that I had experienced but placed in the back of my mind as an unspoken trauma. Other women were victims, which was more disturbing. I immediately contacted the attorney in the article, shared my story, and was the fourth woman of seven women who filed lawsuits against this man, a White man.

I was thrust into a movement against sexual predators and the justice of women victims of sexual violence called the #MeToo movement. I had been silent about the incident for six months until I saw that news article and acquired the courage to step forward for justice for myself and other women. Justice was served.

However, I was still dealing with the trauma of sexual assault and my brother getting shot.

Violence was overbearing. I reflected on violence against Black women and men, especially by the hands of White racists and predators. The fear of being Black in America is real and as I thought about my story in the #MeToo movement, senseless gun violence that my brother survived, and the unarmed killings of Black people by police officers, I wondered "Am I Next?" "Am I the next victim of violence?"

#Am I Next? is an artistic, political, and cultural movement that gives

voice to Black men and women who are victims and survivors of various manifestations of violence. The question is reflective of the person who has experienced trauma and the person who causes it. It opens the wound to address remedies, solutions, and healing through policy reform, Black liberation, and community control.

ripple

every vibration
is
a movement

two sides

either you are pouring
replenishing, restoring
speaking life growth &
abundance

or

you are extracting
taking &
robbing
speaking death only.

so, the question
becomes:

for what cause do
you fight?

                          & to what
                                end?

moves

movement
never stands still & silent; it
only knows
action & voice.

nuff said

cant say
it aint bin sweet

cant say it
aint bin
bitter,
either

but
i can say

dis world sho is
hurtin

somethin

terrible

teal

my skin is black
& love
is in
my heart

beast

these beasts
are their ancestors wildest
dreams

fragmented…
evil
        dangerous, even

that they have claimed us
to be

for

centuries

skin story

The symbols in my skin tell a story
much different from what you
have written who's to say the
blood is a spoken word twice-
told

I can't unzip my skin
African Negro Black Nigga
Criminal
Brute Savage Mandingo Invisible
I can't unzip my skin

From mother Africa metal
coffles-
Cartwhip iron-muzzle-
Bread near-heart-cage-
Middle-passage conductors
this journey, will-be-long

Momma didn't sing no light song
Field hollers all night long on white
cloud cover fields at dawn
the only heartbeat under the moon

& I can feel it running
waking me & baby brother

We hold each other's hands
resilient survivors
Drowning water soul blue ocean
mouth
Bury me now, if you will.
drought is alive & well Ibos
landing & other sanctuary spirit
holders I call your name
I-call-out-your-name
Olaudah Equiano
Phyllis Wheatley
John Brown
Sojourner Truth
Nat Turner
Harriet Tubman
Delia Webster
Frederick Douglass
Charlotte Forten Grimke
Shadows from the Underground

walk trailing along the trees
silence breathing against the
leaves for generations to

become ancestral descendants
painted on timber

Battle wound of flesh
Protest signage "I Am a
Woman" melanated
segregation "I Am a Man"
Canine bloodshed spray
hose lynchings tree
hanging fruit & flowers each
hour under the sky clock is a
decree for protection

I call your name

Emmett Till *the bomb
detonated at 10:19
a.m., killing Cynthia Wesley, Carole
Robertson, Addie Mae
Collins, Denise McNair-* Four
Little Girls
Four Little Girls
Their names deserve to be
spoken aloud

I call your name

Pay homage give somethings for
their sufferings
Give reverence for them
Break their back
Break their neck on that-there
noose
Break the law for unjust rule
Break their heart for mother father
children whose lives were used as
example
Some kind of standard
They walked the middle of frozen
winter-wind for freedom for an
education for a better life for their
families without regret

Please pay some respect
They boarded ships at sick sea
overboard bodies
They squatted their infant child on
their own between their knees
They died for you to speak

What will you leave?
Pay allegiance.

Please pay attention.
Ancestral veneration

We welcome you into this room All
freedom fighters-justice seekers
Sung & unsung heroes of
yesterdays & tomorrows
We welcome you into this room

Men of perseverance We
call your name Malcolm
X
Ralph Abernathy
Jessie Owens
Stokely Carmichael Reverend
Dr. Martin Luther King, Jr.
President Barack Hussein Obama

Women of fortitude We
call your name
Rosa Parks
Audre Lorde
Ruby Bridges
Ella Baker
Coretta Scott King
Angela Davis

Soror Betty Shabazz
First Lady Michelle Obama

First Black man to earn a PhD;
an intellectual scholar –
Dr. W. E. B DuBois

First Black woman millionaire
Sarah Breedlove
You may know her by
"Madam C. J. Walker" She
knew how to work the hot
comb.
Developed her own hair care
products from scratch.
We know how to make
something out of nothing.

Father of Black History Month
Dr. Carter G. Woodson

*Today, I honor-pay homage to my
great-grandfather, Reverend
Thomas Clifford Wells born
January 25, 1882 in Georgia. After
emancipation, the most respected*

job that a Black person could have was to become a preacher or teacher.

Reverend T.C. Wells was one of the first graduates of Morehouse College, a Historically Black College/ University originally named Atlanta Baptist Seminary in Georgia. After graduating, he relocated to Pensacola, Florida with his wife, Annie Campbell, a full-blooded Native American woman from North Carolina, & their children.

Rev. T.C. Wells was one of 15 ministers who organized the church that he & his wife took into their home. Today, Greater Little Rock Baptist Church is a renown-Black megachurch in Pensacola, Florida. & today, I continue in his footsteps as a PhD in Education. I don't take the task lightly. & we shouldn't either. We have work to do. There is work to be done.

Liberation seekers
Justice preservers
We call your name
Kentucky-made

Whitney M. Young
Wilma Rudolph
Muhammad Ali Anne
Braden
Woodford R. Porter
Dr. J. Blaine Hudson Elmer
Lucille Allen Reverend Louis
Coleman, Jr. Michele
Hemenway
Walter Hutchins
Lucille McDonald
You
I
I'm just spitting facts
Telling it like it is
We are of this lineage
Where are you in the
genealogical path-walk
rooted deep on the
family tree?

Ancestors, we are your descendants
We search for you in Bibles,
Slave Schedules,
Photo Albums, Obituaries,
Census records-
legal representatives who visited
your dwelling number but didn't
have the respect to spell your name
correctly

Survivors, under the same sun organ
We stand upon your shoulders
We walk in your stride
We hold strong to the torch
& call out your name
We pay homage

The symbols in my skin tell a story
Much different from what you
have written
who's to say the blood is a
spoken word twice-told…

free

this is my life this is
my breath this is
what I live for
this is what I die for
freedom
freedom to be a woman
freedom to be a man
freedom to be black
freedom to be alive
freedom to protect my joy
viewed as vulnerability
& not the love
I have to give
to this world

biblical

you hate me without reason
for what fear?
for what cause?
this verse
is
familiar

chains

slave
brute
negro
black
cargo
boy
savage

          they name

shackled arrested
killed

          we reclaim

i: am

i am love
beautiful
intelligent
wise
handsome
strong
educated
on the rise.
a child
a woman
a man
human
i
am here

20/20 vision

faith,
focus
&
fast

for fear
leads
only
to
destruction

armed

i got
all this anger
bottled up
in me; ready for
war

tides

just like the river jordan people
are rising I feel the tears falling
as every body falls they say us
empaths can feel the river
rising can feel the moon rising
my heart is heavy but my head
remains high & lifted the energy
the vibe the spirit
must remain nourished
this is the time to revolt this is
the time to revolutionize this is
the time to do the work with
tangible outcomes & goals
just like the tides
we are rising

prayers

lord,

*in this time of
pain, god
keep me &
my family
covered &
protected
amen*

in remembrance

i
call out
i
call out i
call out
your
name…
in remembrance
i
call out
i
call out i
call out
your
name…
in remembrance

in your space

in a world
of hatred
& hard
things

i do hope that
you find

softness
&
sanctuary
in
your
silent
dreams

street love

out here: in these
streets. they dont
love you they dont
love me

transparency

i need you to
show me who
you are
henceforth &
after

rage

i ask for quiet silence
in this rage called war

waves

the ripple
effect
begins
with you

miracle michael

heart of a hero; wisdom
of a wound. soul of a
survivor
we named you miracle,
since the womb

nationalism

i am a woman
who carries a pistol on
one hip
&
a baby on the other
aint i a woman
aint i a mother

song

balance

&

peace: liberation

&

release

low vibrations

it is toxic parasitic
cancerous diseased
when
it
no longer
feels
like
life living
purpose

symphony

create your world
unapologetically

&

let it be refuge
let it be sanctuary
let it be you & God

&

love surrounding

wind

they sayin
another
life has
been
taken

I can feel it.

                                                the

                                          change

                                                  in

                                              the

                                                 air

I can feel it.

phone call

the first response is
not the variations of
"hello" or "hey"
or
"good morning"
the first response is

"where you at?"

…

"you ok?"

living while black

was it an identity
mistaken?
or a mistaken
identity?

mourning

this world is hurting.
its wounds are
bleeding
scabbed but healing
my soul is weeping

#Am I Next?

may the souls of Black folk, living
& rested be lifted & liberated
through love & light, always.
we speak power & strength &
courage upon your name for it has
been written & it is the final
say…
we stand in solidarity, unity, &
peace. White supremacy has only
brought chaos, war, disunity
oppression & poverty, inexcusably.
my hearts in pain & my soul cant
sleep.
I got these feelings that I
cant shake.
do I want revenge
or peace?
we need love in this world. remedy
& release. affirmations. validation.
not anxiety & grief. the last
seconds. the last breath. the last
thoughts, emotions & the memories.

the core center of me the
meditation, prayer, the God in
me cry out on my knees,
momma, wrap me up, hold me
please now a candlelight vigil.
airbrushed t-shirt.
obituary ceremonial rebirth Im
steady cryin for this world. I got
hope & Im tryin Im steady
survivin in this world. but I still
aint thrivin they say there's two
types of Black people in this
world: the peaceful
&
riot. we one of the same. we
just trynna stop from dying.
Am I next?
   Ahmaud Arbery.
Am I next?
   George Floyd.
Am I next?
   Breonna Taylor.
Am I next?
   David McAtee. trynna put
death on my name but God
designed a masterpiece. still the

question remains: how many
killings? how many deaths?
how many murders will it take
before you choose who's next?
life & time, now that's divine
connection, still you seek to
bereave. just cause I was
protesting? just cause I was
progressing?
Im just confessing.
just cause I advocate for the
community.
you choose to take my
immunity? everything
I own.
you try to cop from me.
everything that has life but Im
breaking free. we need laws in
place that protect the people,
see. we need Black control,
independence, agency
Im honest.
we need respect, understanding,
transparency.
Imma tell you who we are & who
we aint gon be.

this is crazy; how many times
will we repeat history? a cycle
of dysfunction manifesting
generationally.
I cant breathe.
Aint I a Woman?
I Am a Man.
Black Lives Matter! That's the
new age eulogy you shot me at
least eight time while I slept on
the couch. you broke in &
entered into my house.
searching for someone already
locked down. innocent
bystander how many more
Black bodies will we count?
Im still trynna figure why you
pulled that trigger was it 'cause Im
a black person you named a nigger
Imma call it what it is. police
patrol is white control. the first
slave catchers were on the slave
masters payroll. they come into
our neighborhoods collecting
souls. Black bodies are
expendable to you is what I know.
now you here with each bullet fired.

you play a role they dont want me
in this america. I aint lived yet.
protect the people my question is
who you gon' kill next?
blood crime scene gun vest. police
call it protection. toting a murder
weapon killing every black face
they trynna teach a lesson hate
crimes are jealousy, but I got
blessings my heart tells me to heal,
but my mind is still vetting me you
still on the streets living life, for
this case, there aint no plea aint no
bargain for a life, no justice no
peace
I'll march in the streets & fight
til the death of me I'll protect
what's mine & my
right to breathe put my life on
the line for my family
& I'll do it with integrity
& loyalty til this
oppression cease,
since on this soil we been
everything but human beings.
Im taking back what belongs to me

this is chess not checkers, its all in
the strategy we demand justice &
change for the community placed
in the right people's hands. we
have a case that we are seeking
legitimizing black lives on this
land; my heart is King. my mind
is Malcolm. my soul spreads
peace while my spirit sings an
anthem; I cant rest
theres too much unrest & a knee
against my neck I can't breathe is
the plea but to blue blood
I digress;
Im praying for our lives;
Im claiming victory;
Im trynna do things right, but
you got a bullet on my life
I got hope & healing
I got faith
Im willing to talk it through but
now you got me chanting hands up
dont shoot they say Im too
conscious for savages

your appetite dont lie to you. listen
to your gut. Im hungry for the
living truth
you took that heartbeat away from
me. You left his body on the
streets
you have no regard for human life-
Black lives including me.
Am I next? Will self-hatred get the
best of you in moments of distress?
I wont sleep until these animals are
off the street.
we gotta have our own. Be a
voice in this fever-heat
It hits different when the
memorial is for your peeps. all I
can think is that could have
been me... I put my life on the line.
I'm armed up with my arms up you
cant take what's mine. say her
name. say his name movement
requires a plan.
execution. preparation tactics for
retribution. we need a healing not
hell in this world of Black
persecution turn anger into action.
turn pain into protest. turn rage

into revolution. I say this in the Creator's name. stay blessed. Amen.

to the church

healing
is in
the
heart
mend that first

& then:
you can come talk to me

peculiar & ripe

we need a healing from within
war is unnecessary but if you
bring the strap best believe we
won't be sedentary protection
safety we trynna spare our
babies aint no hands up don't
shoot your hand is off the
safety trigger happy officers
that's where your hate is you
declared a civil war
criminalizing Black skin

there's nothing else to loose
all I see is me you got goons we got
shooters at the scene we can't trust
the police *black bodies falling in the*
southern breeze
this strange fruit
she weeps for her son
under the sun his body
lifeless in the middle of
the street

bag em up they see us as
commodities if they take
something from me then you
know im bringing heat

on the line we stay woke
with dreams while we
keep our hand on the
time

divine

trust
God's alignment
&
God's timing
cause in every
lesson
there is a blessing
in every blessing
there is a lesson

homage

ancestors never
complained kept
rioting kept
marching kept
lifting

planted firmly
in the ground
work

        I am who ancestors pray
                                       &
                        fight for

ancestors

I prayed
I prayed for you
I prayed

broken open

we have to stay focused on the vision & God's plan. there are many important messages in the time that we're in. have to stay in divine alignment for enlightenment

sanctuary

am in my world & you trying
touch my heart & soul
trying to get in touch the center
core
get to the inner of me & I let
you in every time I let you in
let you touch the soft spaces
tender places vulnerability
the religion in me
I let you in like I let in
God
let you see let you taste
the nectar the ripe
unseen parts

desire

you love me
soft & sweet
when life is
hard & bitter
& I thank
you for that

in the soul sacred of this place
where my heart dwells
all I want is love in this world is
that too much to ask?
is that too much?

fake

i taught you
my religion &:

you took it

origin

she warrior
goddess
light sense the beginning of
time like mother who gives
life just before her time she
was born, as well always
manifesting seeding
abundance growth for
new moon cycle
& sunrise

frontline

we need warriors & if you aint on
the same frequency
we cant do the work united
we cant do the power driven
purpose love
we cant do the work together

veneration

channeling all
these
spirits from
ancestors
resting among roses
&
elders who still can smell
them

chosen

&
she
led
the
people

this hate: similar

i carried you
out: protected
you.

      thats what loyalty means

you aint agree
      you gave
      my name
      to the streets

when i see you

      keep. that. same. energy.

sun tribe

bronze
red brown
cream black
yellow
golden sun
orbit skin
color hair
wrapped
sage burning
sistahs

s.h.e.

womanhood is power
empathy rising in
womb resting on
shoulders straddling
against back hitting
high on thighs
i carry children
promises
of tomorrow
&
spirit of
yesterday

ti(iii)red

aint no mo in me

i aint gon keep
on
keepin on

im tired
bin tired

when we
movin on?

she & he

I am only human
goddess & god divine balance
divinity with superhuman
capabilities heroic flawless
qualities but just a soul with a
heart who speaks against the
silent wings that pat the sky at
night & beat the drum by day
i am only human

but,
again

*that's just
what they
say*

moves

water anxious overpour

all energy vibes
i can feel its intentions
& reservations
spoken &
silent

ready & willing to do what
needs to be done all in the
name of justice revolution
new age synergy

in the quest to find
what's missing

still complete

i am peace in
a world of
pieces

lift me

sun an orange
orbit halo
energy
synchronicity
all vibrations
reminders
we are here
still in time cant get that 2:37pm
back from yesterday already
passed
all we got is presence
now & each other

stay woke

that's my place to be
i speak for the pack
while the wolves
stay asleep

awaken

orange resting warm
against my face
beautiful sunrise
woke up today
weather downpour
rain or blue-sky
ocean will run with
you into the horizon
if it rests in you
illuminating

blessings

this life world
is priceless but it's
worth so much
it's worth so much
yet it's
priceless

presence

I see you

&

I know:

you are here

always

just near

thank you,

for being softness against
my wounds

warrior

i got
wounds
healed &
unhealed

scars
seen
&
unsee
n

learned

                    i knew you
would come back trynna
swoon me put on a face
        dress differently tell
      me
    you learned
  read new words
 down for the movement but
you aint learned
you aint did shit different
 same shit like always
 this all a game a cycle
 that i done seen already
   you aint change

ride or die

& when the world fears you & kills
you i will hold you in my arms &
wrap you up i will hold & kiss
your face remove the tears from
the breath of you hold you like a
mother sister cousin who loves you
immensely & i will lie down with
you whether on concrete ground on
your living room couch in the
hospital wing-south i will die with
you because that's real love that's
real love true i will do that i will
do that for you if nobody else will

movement

that's the movement
call mission vision
& center of you.

hate

that orange sun keeps me moving
my heart a beating drum to breathe
& seed
nothing but life & love to give
that's all that is in me
still you fear me
for what?
for what cause?
to what end?

sincerely,

> beautiful sunrise,
> love

still waiting

Black people
are the most
forgiving
beings on this
planet on
this side
of the cosmos

*who else out there better
than us?*

(w) supremacy

></>enslave

>miseducate

>incarcerate

>hate

>yeah:
>you hate
>real good.

kkk:
killers, kops & korona

its either them or me kkk
keep flexin
they drop bodies we
drop bodies
to teach a lesson
we put a bounty on your head
we got blue blood on our hands I
know this day will make history.
every life taken
that's a bounty on your
peace is my philosophy
I can't sleep until the cops who took
his life says I can't breathe. we need
trained warriors, nationalists for the
cause.
I stand & fight any white
nationalist hog.
you got hunters
we got killers
that's a number on
your head nigga

peace is what we
want & deserve not
countless black
lives dead, if
you bring a war ammunition, best
believe we pumping bullets in
your chest.
don't get me wrong I got peace in
my heart but when you mess with
one of mine I got a choppa go that
part. Black lives
they want us exterminated
blood stained in the streets
aint no getting life back without
your name on the lease
you get life or life taken.
that's the name of the streets
sorry apologize for what?
being black? skin
criminalize
police traumatize
they made me like this.

life is

I can breathe
I can see
I can speak

I am free

we want peace not war
but if you bring your gun
I'll bring the heat.

we got enemies & allies
we got advocates on sidelines
we got warriors & soldiers
willing & ready for revolt &
rise.

seen this before

"america
is
falling."

        an elder told me

the impact is
greater
much greater
than

rome

this time
'round

choices

lotta people
                                        sleeping

lotta people
                                        dreaming

lotta people
                                        dying

lotta people
                                        bleeding

young wonder

fri. may 29, 10:38 pm

news flash on t.v:

after hearing that multiple unarmed black people have been recently murdered by the police, a Black girl & boy lie across the bed in their own thoughts. the girl rests on her stomach & turns to the boy.

girl: *what are you thinking?*

the boy is lying on his back with one arm under his head staring blankly at the ceiling. not breaking his stare, he hesitates before answering.

boy: *what if we're dreaming? what if this is all a dream?* silence sets in between them before the girl speaks.

girl: *maybe, this is just one of the many lives that we will live.*

the boy responds confidently.

boy: *if it is, then I hope it's not the best one.*

the girl stares off into the deep abyss of her mind as silence spills into the room until the boy turns to the girl & asks a question.

boy: *what are you thinking?*

girl: *that maybe one day, a long time from now, we will remember & feel this exact moment in time.*

the room dims into the night, traveling into the cosmos.

About the Author

Dr. Tytianna Nikia Maria Ringstaff, Founder, and CEO of Honey Tree Publishing is the author and publisher of more than 7 books. As an author and educator, she teaches classes and develops curriculum for Pre-K through 12th grade schools and higher education institutions. Dr. Ringstaff holds a Ph.D. in Curriculum and Instruction from the University of Louisville. She enjoys traveling the world with her husband and family.

www.ingramcontent.com/pod-product-compliance
Lightning Source LLC
Chambersburg PA
CBHW070435010526
44118CB00014B/2058